CU00792671

MAYBE ANOTHER TIME WHEN I´M NOT WATCHING TV!

Whatever happened to spontaneity? Do we really have to arrange two weeks in advance to talk about the weather with someone or at worst be frightened to even ask for fear of rejection? What is this world coming to!

MAYBE ANOTHER TIME WHEN I´M NOT WATCHING TV!

Grit

ARTHUR H. STOCKWELL LTD.
Torrs Park   Ilfracombe   Devon
Established 1898
www.ahstockwell.co.uk

British Library Cataloguing-in-Publication Data.
A catalogue record for this book is available
from the British Library.

By the same author:
Natural Woman

ISBN 978-0-7223-3831-5
Printed in Great Britain by
Arthur H. Stockwell Ltd.
Torrs Park   Ilfracombe
Devon

Contents

SO BLACK

My soul.
My knickers.
My coffee.
My humour.
My limousine.
My karate belt.
My hole.
My list.
My eye.
My book.
My berry pie.
My sheep.
My pudding.
My velvet in the tall / slim glass.
My mark.

PRESTO!

What with
fast food and
fast forward and
fast pace and
fast finish and
fast lane and
fast love,
isn´t there anything we do slowly any more?
We do.
We slowly unravel the complete and utter mess
we made by doing everything so fast in the first place!
Otherwise known as "engage brain a while first
before throwing yourself into the throng."

A QUICK STORY

The *throaty* man who was the heart-*throb* of almost every woman in the kingdom (united or not), was in the *throes* of an act of indulgence when he had a *thrombosis* and fell gravely ill. People were subsequently worried about the state of the *throne*. Word of this via the grapevine fell on the King´s ears (in the royal hospital bed), who then *threw* himself into the *throng* to put the record straight, and consequently proceeded to *throttle* the person who spread the slanderous rumours in the first place. *Through* all the trials and tribulations and *throughout* the realm his *throughput* was quite undefeated. He was certainly not going to give them the chance to *throw* him out that easily and to *throwaway* his hard work over years.

The moral of the story is: when you´re hoarse avoid being ridden like one!

P.S. Order of appearance by courtesy of the dictionary (throaty thru throwaway).

BAD BOT BUSTS BALL

"Bad Bot Busts Ball".
Some headline.
The story is that
you´re bad and you´ve bust my ball.
I certainly should be having one.
You´re bad that´s for sure.
You´re a bot ´cos you don´t
have feelings, like them.
You´ve bust my ball
´cos I can´t buy the clothes to wear to it.
And my suitor won´t
show till you go.

Conclusion: Better Buy Big Bullets

BAD, BAD, BAD BOYS

Bad boys batter babies.
Beautiful babies belong battered.
Bad boys belong buried!

CLOTHES THAT MAKE

The devil wears Prada.
And the angel? – M&S.
And the junky? – The same thing day in, day out.
And the thief? – Other people´s.
And the homeless? – A bin liner if need be.
And the best mummy (according to her kids)
who is up to her ears in probs
of a financial kind? – Goods on sale, sale, sale, sale!

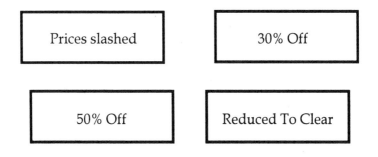

Prices slashed	30% Off
50% Off	Reduced To Clear

P.S. We all have the devil in us, but we don´t
all (need to) have Prada on us!

RELEASED

Anyone can "fall by the wayside".
Important is to get back "on track" again.
Easier said than done in some cases.
But it´s worth the try.
There´s nothing to lose but the

Time you had   ′   O

Time you did   X

$$\$$$

Time you have left   ?

$$\$$$

EROTIC

Are you watching me
watching you?
Are you watching me
eyeing you?
Are you watching me
feeling you?
Are you watching me
kissing you?
Are you watching me
licking you?
Are you watching me
and my hands all over you?
Are you watching me
f * * * * * * you?

Watch me!

PRESERVE

Save the planet.
Save for a rainy day.
Save me that.
Screen save.
Save time.
Save your breath.
Save-all.
Save space.
Save our souls.
Save appearances.
Save nine (9) with a stitch in time.
Save as you earn.
Well, if I had a job, I would . . . .

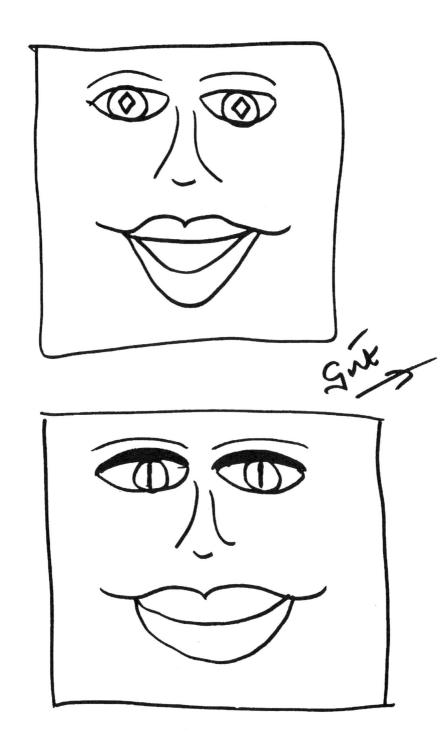

OPUS

O	–	operatic
P	–	performance
U	–	under
S	–	stars

As in "Vaida" in Verona!

HIT THE JACKPOT

I arrived between the 23rd and the 21st.
I´m passionate, courageous,
accountable and autonomous.
And my injection is painful.
What am I?

INTELLIGENCE / LOVE / SEX

My *intelligence* tells me that there
is more to true *love* than just *sex*.

My *intelligence* tells me that just
love and no *sex* is truly boring . . . .

FRANK (WITH OURSELVES)

That´s how we are,
you and I.
We say what we mean,
    get straight down to it.
There are no frills and bows,
        no starters, just main course.
What you see is what you get!
So trust me as I so want to trust you . . . .

DESPERATE

I want you like I´m gasping for the last breath of air on this
planet. I want you . . . .

THE MAN IN THE BAGGY SHIRT

Didn't notice him at first, the man in the baggy shirt.
Where did *he* come from?
There he was in front of me, that cool guy.
We exchanged looks, loaded.
I smiled briefly.
We moved our bodies in time.
The floor was getting hot.
We moved towards each other.
And then together – wow!
Fast, too fast – take it slow,
use that rhythm.
Hot, much hotter now.
His strong hands steering my hips.
Desire arousing and . . . .

He dumped me for an SMS!

OFFERING

Walking around looking like Santa Claus
just before Xmas was fun!
But quite frankly I do it every day . . . .
I always bear gifts!

PREOCCUPIED

I have a lot on my mind right now –
your alluring eyes, your tender lips,
your golden mane . . . .
A tingle down my spine which lingers . . . .
A warmth in my veins which spreads . . . .
A love in my heart which bonds.

BATTLEAXE BARBARA´S BATTERED BABY

Battleaxe Barbara baked bread.
Barbara´s beautiful baby blinked.

Battleaxe Barbara belongs battered.
Battleaxe Barbara belongs buried!

Boys brought big bat.
Boys battered Barbara´s baby.

Barbara´s battered baby bleeds.
Barbara buried battered baby.

Boys battered Barbara´s belly.
Boys buried Barbara´s body.

Bad boys belong buried.
Batman bought big bat.

Batman battered bad boys.
Boys buried by batman.

J L S

Jill   likes soul,
loves sex,
likes spaghetti,
loves Stefan (SE)?
likes silk,
loves sun (sand & sea),
likes scary movies,
loves swimming,
likes snowfall,
loves singing,
likes sincerity,
loves sailing,
likes sky blue,
loves sensual moments.

MIGRAINE

It causes throbbing in what´s known
as the frothy part of a pint of Guinness.
It affects one side.
It makes you throw up.
It limits your vision.
It can go on for days.
It can ruin your plans.
It can be eased with tablet (most probably several).

Thank goodness I´m not prone!

THE X-LINES

Thanx. . . . .for a nice summer.

Trix	–	He often has a bag of trix with him.
Mix	–	He likes to mix at those trendy parties.
Fix	–	Jim liked to fix it.
Six	–	Don´t put all those six eggs in one basket.
Pix	–	She always pix her friends badly.
Lix	–	He lix his ice cream until it runs.
Tix	–	The clock tix so fast when you´re having fun.
Kix	–	He kix that football as straight as a dye.
Nix	–	Often trousers sit better without nix.
Vix	–	That vix nasal spray almost blows your head off.
Wix	–	Those candles have unbelievably long wix, they burn forever!

MISSING LIMB

When you left that day
a part of me went with you.
I need it back . . . .
I (just) need you.

YOU CAN CALL ME

Hi, it´s me.
I felt like talking to you.
But I just knew it was going
to be your answering machine!
Actually I´d prefer to talk to *you*.
The good thing is that you
now have my voice on tape,
which is what you wanted!
It can never be a substitute
for the real thing though . . . .
Bye.

APPEARANCE

Love never says when it is coming.
What if it´s the wrong place?
What if it´s the wrong time?
What if it´s too late?
What if it came and went . . . .
never to return?!

TO SANTA (WISH LIST)

Wish list for Xmas 2006:
New Year celebrations – Home Alone.
Do hope it´s not going to be
"the same procedure as last year Ms Holdsworth."
And I didn´t even have any absent ones present!
Thanks in advance.

DON'T YOU WISH . . . .

She was. . . .

    h
wrong like me,
    t

     w
a freak like me,
     a
     k (for you)

right like me?
    o
    r
    n
    y

SELF-ASSURANCE

I don´t know what confidence means.
My little darling it means
believing in yourself,
going your own way,
not letting others push you about,
being firm when needed,
speaking your mind,
asking for what you need,
choosing what you like,
asking questions,
ignoring scorn,
listening to your inner voice.

SHE LOVES ME – SHE LOVES ME NOT

She loves me.
She helps me.
She pitys me.
She mocks me.
She hates me.

She loves me not.
She helps me not.
She pitys me not.
She mocks me not.
She hates me not.

Who is she?
I don´t know her from Adam!

FOLK

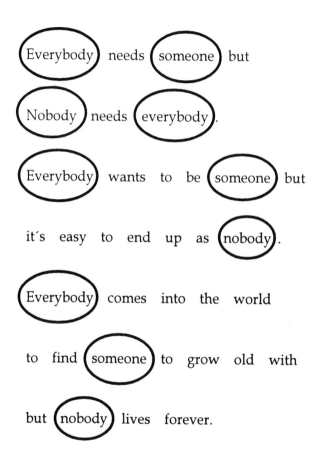

Everybody needs someone but
Nobody needs everybody.
Everybody wants to be someone but
it's easy to end up as nobody.

Everybody comes into the world
to find someone to grow old with
but nobody lives forever.

THE OTHER SIDE OF THE GLASS

Snow dunes upon snow dunes.
Dots of light.
The noble Xmas tree firmly planted.
A car now and then.
A kind of hush all over (the town).
Plus one.
A heavy sky.
A lingering of firework smoke
following an array of a splendid kind.
The dawning of a new year with
all its hopes and fears for any of us.

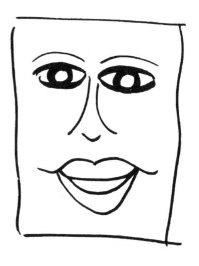

YOU FREAK ME OUT

Don't make me beg.
Don't take me down a peg.
But you do!
Everytime I see you.
That's far and few between.
Sadly, but maybe still for the best.

But I need yours, not his, tonight.
You enter this joint as a threesome.
We could leave as a twosome.
But you won't!
You time it just right (wrong).
"F * * * him," she shouts out from the corner.
Given half a chance . . . .
But you will not with me!
Repeat performances can be a bore.
So, bye for now (and the next).

PC – PER**X**ONAL COMP**X**TER PROBLEM CHILD

You are charged with being in a state
of "excessive happiness".
Oh, good gracious.
What now?
For how long?
Well, I did say I´d like to
get away from it all!
Not quite the ticket.
A change of wallpaper.
But from grey to bright floral,
not vice versa!
What´s wrong with being happy anyway?
Even if it is I-N-X-S!
The lead singer of that band
certainly did . . . . overdo things!
If I´m to be branded a nuisance
for "dancing out of line" then
I´ll live with it and I´m *proud* to
say that I have the *courage* to do both.
It´s a rare breed of (wo)men without
which the world would have perished long since.

OVERINDULGENCE

Hope you made that shopping spree!
Hope you had a lovely time.
Hope you squandered.
Hope it was considerable.
Hope you got yourself something nice.
Just in case you didn´t . . . .
Here´s a little something from me.

Par Avion

...... HIGH ......

I´m arrogant if I´m "high and mighty".
I´m stranded if I´m "on high".
I´m greater than average in height with a "high collar".
It´s at its peak when it´s "high noon".
I´m elated and cheerful when I´m in "high spirits".
I´m very important when I´m a "high priestess".
I´m a great distance above sea when
I´m standing on a "high plateau".
It´s of great intensity when it´s a "high wind".
My life´s luxurious when it´s a "high" one.
I´m expressing contempt when I´m using "high words".
I´m exalted in style when I´m in "high drama".
It´s acute in tone when "high (in) pitch".
It´s favourable to have a "high opinion".
I often clock up that "high mileage".
It´s advanced in complexity that "high finance".
I´m specified when I´m "3-feet high".
It´s performed @ an elevation that "high dive".
I´m at a specified level when I´m
"knee high" . . . . to a grasshopper!

FIGHTING FOR YOURS

Life's too short and sometimes bitter.
Shorter for some than others.
Make yours as sweet as you can,
for *as long as you can*.

TWO'S COMPANY, THREE'S A CROWD

Jill The Pill	-	She's a "pick-me-up".
Josh The Cosh	-	He's a "troublemaker".
Jordan The Warden	-	She's "keeping everyone in order".

But, it works when you're in the right one . . . .

REFUSAL

Her: Do you want to come round?
Him: Sorry, maybe another time.
        Sorry, maybe when I´m not watching TV.
        Sorry, maybe when I´m not alone.
Her: No!
        Sorry, maybe next lifetime!

MAKING AMENDS

Even when you have done something very "wrong"
there is still a chance to do something "right"
for someone, somewhere, somehow . . . .
All it takes is a small step –
to take the initiative.

THE GAME

Life is rather like a football match in many ways.
One meets those of both an offensive
and defensive kind along the way.
One has to be on one's guard
for "fierce" competition and unfair play.
One has to think "team" but
being forward is a plus.
There are also those who are
forever judging us.
One has goals to meet.
And the bottom line –
you win some, you lose some.

TRANSFER

She's had pain for as long as I can remember.
And now it's our turn to suffer (the loss).
We all have to go sometime!
But where to?
To a better life (?).
Well, let's hope it's
one without a needle this time.
May she be free of discomfort.
May she be free to choose her culinary bite.
May she be free to enjoy a glass
of whatever she pleases.
May she be free from the rigid daily routine.

May she now . . . . . rest in peace.

PROTECTION

"I was lucky to get this, Mummy," you said.
Thank you.
Well, only me and God really
know what I´ve gone through
for you, my little cherub.
"Any mother would have done it," they say.
Well, maybe . . . . . no!
You need nerves of steel to fight
this (g**X**d) fight.
Constantly thinking "worst-case scenario".
Preventing the "negativity" of yourself.
Finding a "surprise" when you turn every corner.
And forever being able to say:
"I told you so," is not my idea of fun!
Yours?

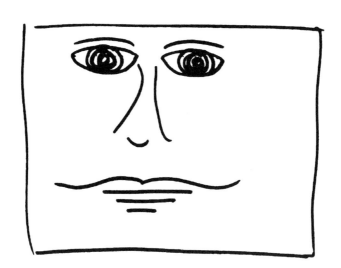

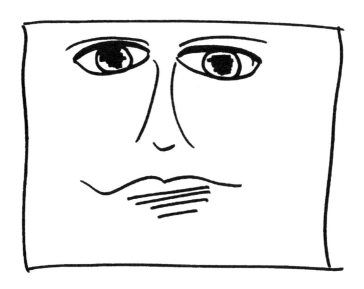

CORE

Their values are my values.
But they still won´t give me a job!
Just what does it take?
To pick up the phone – done that.
To be open and friendly – are that.
To submit an impressive CV – done that.
To be fluent in Norwegian – are that.
To tender good referees – done that.
To be prepared to start any time – are that.
You tell me!

BACKSTAGE

Behind the curtain that spanned for metres they were in full swing. How they just loved to *rehearse*. And this was the last one. That they would have to re-house the theatre within the week was a worry. *Anyhow,* they´d have to put it to the back of their minds. "The show must go on," was on everyone's lips. The little boy in uniform from the house over the road was doing his best to look through the *keyhole*. What is this *unholy* lot doing in the church hall he was asking himself?! The *alcohol* was in everyone's glass in the break. It all felt so good. Why didn´t they realise *beforehand* that this was going to be such a huge success . . . . ? ! ? !   The End.

YOU
(T~~H~~E K~~IN~~G) AND I

You´re after my own **heart**.
She broke his **heart**.
He´s eating his **heart** out.
I´ve got my **heart** in the right place.
You lost **heart**.
She has her **heart** in her mouth.
He wears his **heart** on his sleeve.
I do it with all my **heart**.
You took it to **heart**.
She lost her **heart** to him.
He knew it all by **heart**.
I have the **heart** to do it.
I l-o-v-e you from the bottom of my .... **heart.**

OR WAS IT "DO THE HUSTLE"?

Do the bump!
And I don't mean as the song suggests.
I mean – zap it!
Don't want that growing out of all proportion . . . . .
Oh, and by the way –
it's bad enough having
to fight to preserve your life,
but how would you like to
settle up for it afterwards?!
Not private, not at all costs.
But I was not going to pay with *it*.
No time to lose.
Couldn't wait to go National.
Didn't want my son of early years
to forget me that quick.

UP ON THINGS

"The more you know, the less you feel."

With regard to having some good luck	-	no.	
With regard to career	-	yes.	
With regard to receiving bad news	-	no and yes	
		you´re sympathetic.	you´re numb.
With regard to happenings of a fatal kind	-	yes.	
With regard to your state of health	-	no and yes.	

U dig this 2 ?

GIVE AND TAKE

You gave.
It was taken!
No one knows why???
Pain beyond compare.
It´s make or break.
Cry a lot. Hug a lot.
Kiss a lot. Love a lot.
Make it!
The answer?
There is none.
Just to . . . . . give again (???).

THE BUSY ARTIST

You observe.
You concentrate.
You focus.
You sketch.
You brush.
You smear.
You outline.
You highlight.
You fine-tune.

You capture.
You portray.
You centre.
You exaggerate.

You arouse.
You excite.
You provoke.
You enlighten.

ICE BABY

They slither over the ice

at Rockefeller Centre.

They sip an ice - cold drink in Barbados.

They pack salmon in ice in Alaska.

She´s as cold as ice according to that "Foreigner".

They put ice on their nails by the gallon in Paris.

They´re on thin ice when they´re out on that limb.

We´re breaking the ice whilst we´re making a start

(to get to know . . . .).

WE COME AND GO

When we come into this world it´s painful for some.
When we leave this world it´s painful for others.
You see we leave our mark in some form or shape.
You, NORMAN, exercised the vocal cords
of the likes of many like me.
With aspirations of becoming something,
as so often at that young age.
Still the look of nonchalance on your face
as your fingers slide over those minstrel keys
fresh in my mind.
Week in, week out, you entertained us,
you enthused us, you drilled us,
you frustrated yourself over us.

We never know when it´s time
to go out that door.
Sorry to hear you couldn´t
stay a while longer . . . .

MALE DESCENDANT

My son is the only one (right now)
who **really** understands me.
Once joined by a cord.
Now united in thought,
word and feeling.
Bonded for life – his as mine.
A little man with lots of brain power
and gut feeling.

REACTION

Making someone hate me
is the last thing on this earth
I want.
But I always do.
Just being myself creates
the (un)desired effect!
A fact of (my) life . . . .

THE WHOLE CABOODLE

"What do you want from him?"
Everything.
But true love asks for nothing!
And it was . . . . (genuine).
I didn´t get anything actually.
I wasn´t out for money or such.
Just wanted "the whole story".
The thread to the needle.
The ins and the outs . . . .
of the man I most wanted
to kiss that night.

PAY BACK

You only get what you give.
It´s that simple!
"I, I who have nothing,"
hasn´t given yet, Ms Bassey.
But it´s never too late.
So, give a lot and
you´ll get a lot.
Sooner rather than later!

CHANCE

Opportunity knocks but once!?
But there´s not just one!
There are many . . . .
Keep knocking!
Given the right "break"
I´ll open my door.

SOUND ADVICE
(TO MY SON)

"The more I learn about women
the more I like my motorcycle."
I sure know where he´s coming from.
Women really do suck!
Might seem strange coming from one.
One bad experience follows another.
You can count the species of
a "decent" female kind on 2 hands.
So for starters that´s me, my mum,
my daughter and . . . . . where´s the rest?
Take a long hard look
before you decide, my boy.
The truth is unkind.
But don´t let them be *that* with *you*.
Make sure those around you are
o.k. and not **u.k.**

APPETITE

Are you hungry?

For what?

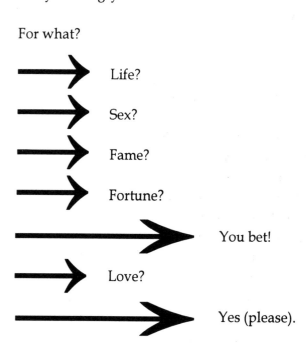

Life?

Sex?

Fame?

Fortune?

You bet!

Love?

Yes (please).

DRIVE

You´re (energy)!
o   I
u   t
r (energy) is (a)(mazing)
            m
            a
            z   A
            e   n
            s (everyone) d
                        o
                 t (everyone) has it!

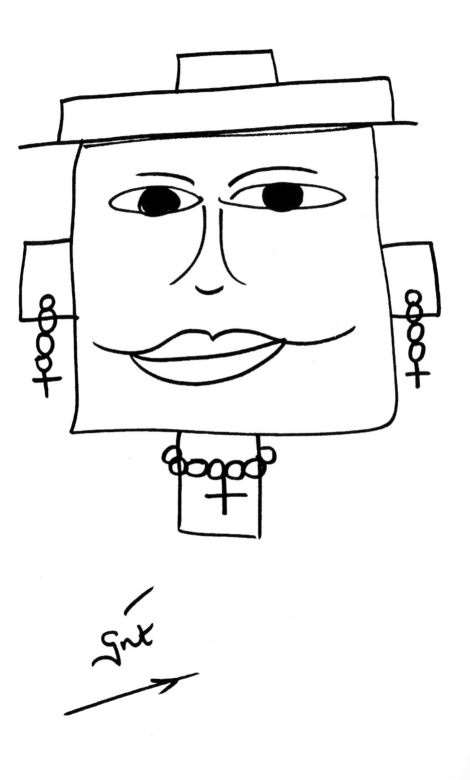